The Beard Coloring Book

Illustrated by Meggyn Pomerleau

Microcosm Publishing | Portland, Oregon

THE BEARD COLORING BOOK

All content © Meggyn Pomerleau

This edition © Microcosm Publishing 2016

The typeface used in this book is Cooper Black.

For a catalog, write

Microcosm Publishing

2752 N. Williams Ave

Portland, OR 97227

or visit MicrocosmPublishing.com

ISBN 978-1-62106-995-9

This is Microcosm #225

Distributed worldwide by Legato / Perseus and in the UK by Turnaround

This book was printed on post-consumer paper in the United States.

Global labor conditions are bad, and our roots in industrial Cleveland in the 70s and 80s made us appreciate the need to treat workers right. Therefore, our books are **MADE IN THE USA.**

I would like to thank the hundreds of burritos that inspired me, motivated me, and maintained my energy throughout the creation of this book (in addition to the aesthetically superior men, women, and animals that follow).

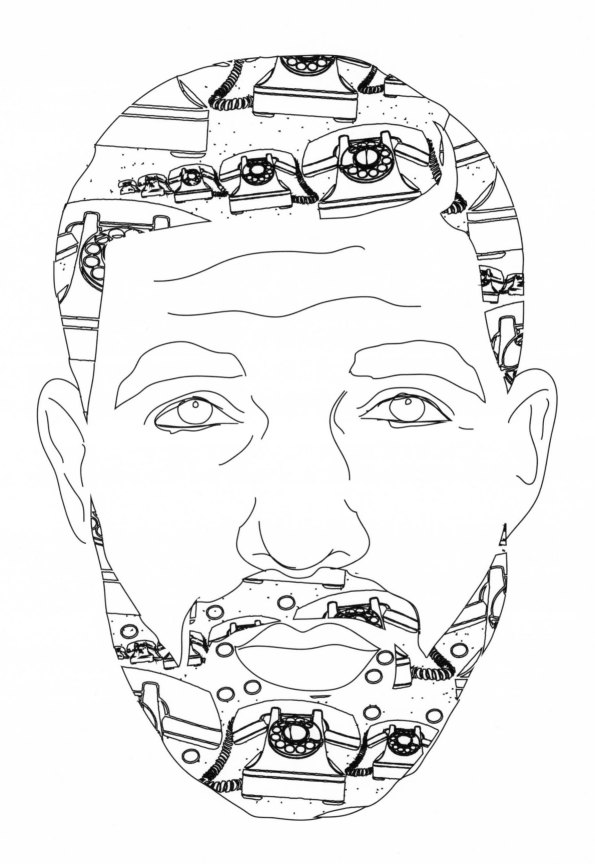

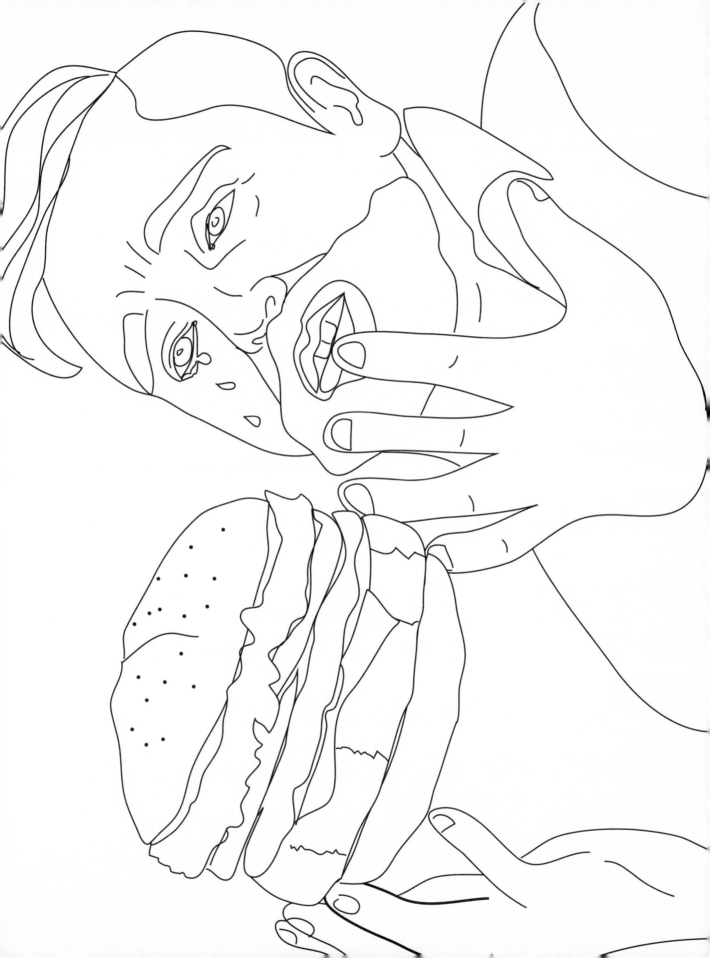

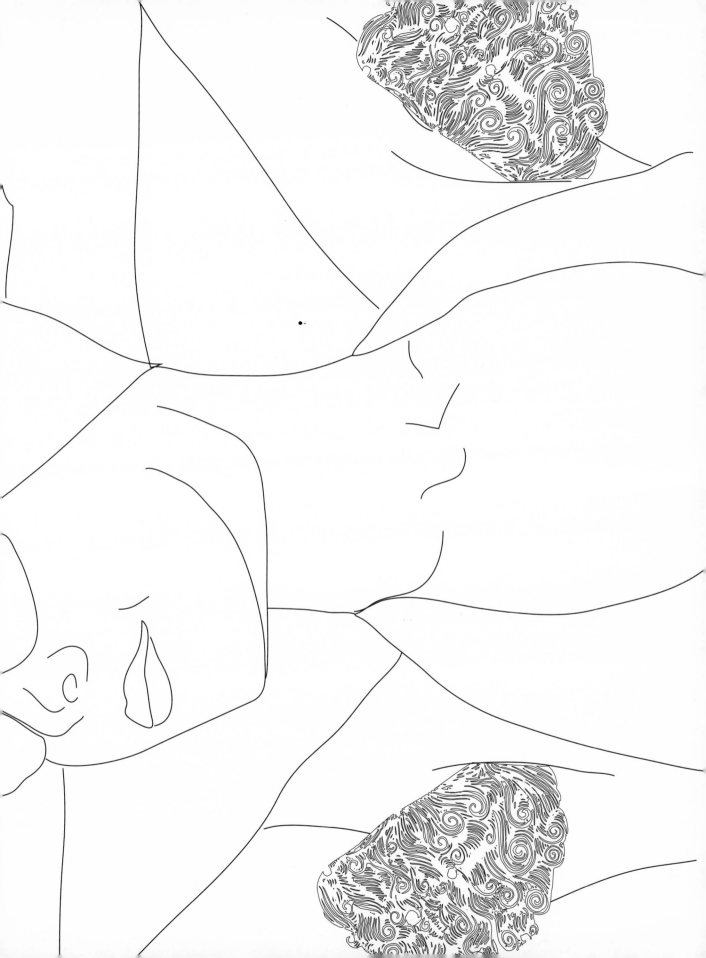

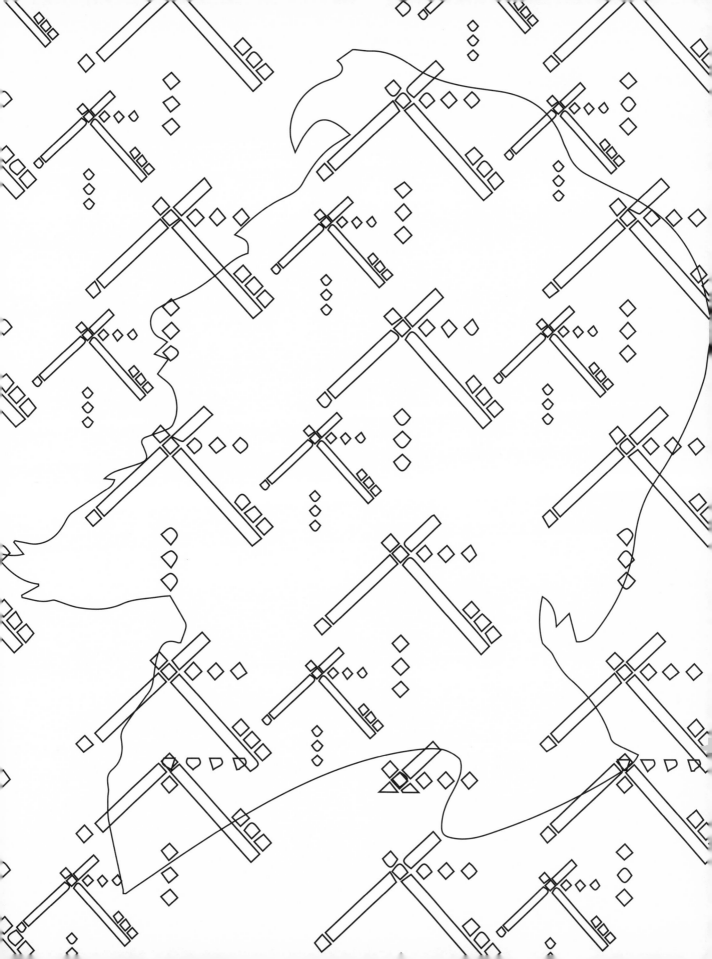

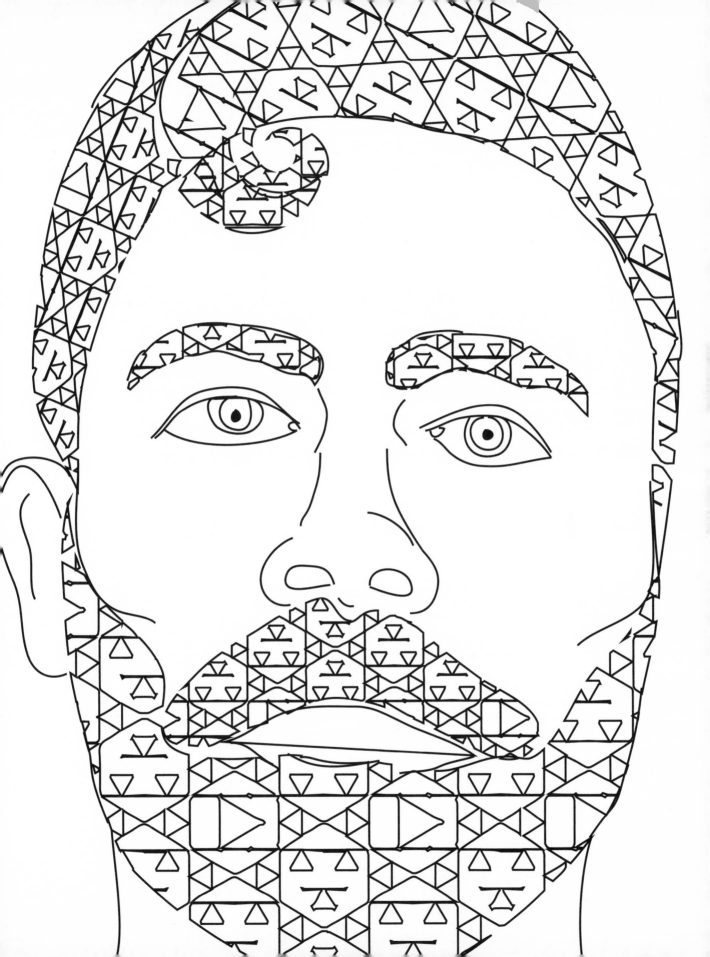

SUBSCRIBE TO EVERYTHING WE PUBLISH!

Do you love what Microcosm publishes?

Do you want us to publish more great stuff?

Would you like to receive each new title as it's published?

Subscribe as a BFF to our new titles and we'll mail them all to you as they are released!

$10-30/mo, pay what you can afford. Include your t-shirt size and month/date of birthday for a possible surprise! Subscription begins the month after it is purchased.

microcosmpublishing.com/bff

...AND HELP US GROW YOUR SMALL WORLD!

More gifts for the discerning radical person in your life:

    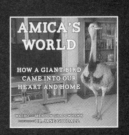